BROKEN RECORDS

BODY RECORDS

TO PUMP YOU UP!

KENNY ABDO

Fly!
An Imprint of Abdo Zoom
abdobooks.com

abdobooks.com

Published by Abdo Zoom, a division of ABDO, P.O. Box 398166, Minneapolis, Minnesota 55439.

Printed in the United States of America, North Mankato, Minnesota.
052023
092023

THIS BOOK CONTAINS RECYCLED MATERIALS

Photo Credits: Alamy, AP Images, Getty Images, Shutterstock
Production Contributors: Kenny Abdo, Jennie Forsberg, Grace Hansen
Design Contributors: Candice Keimig, Neil Klinepier, Laura Graphenteen

Library of Congress Control Number: 2022946929

Publisher's Cataloging-in-Publication Data

Names: Abdo, Kenny, author.
Title: Body records to pump you up! / by Kenny Abdo
Description: Minneapolis, Minnesota : Abdo Zoom, 2024 | Series: Broken records | Includes online resources and index.
Identifiers: ISBN 9781098281380 (lib. bdg.) | ISBN 9781098282080 (ebook) | ISBN 9781098282431 (Read-to-me ebook)
Subjects: LCSH: Records--Juvenile literature. | History--Juvenile literature. | Human body--Juvenile literature.
Classification: DDC 032.02--dc23

TABLE OF CONTENTS

BODY RECORDS

The human body is an incredible thing. But what some people can do with their body is out of this world!

NEURO
RECOR
2020
RE 2020 -
RELOS (59

From longest mustaches to heaviest dead lifts, these world records will pump anyone up!

ELEIKO
25
25

BROKEN RECORDS

Robert Wadlow was named the tallest man in history in 1955. He stood 8 ft 11 in (2.72 m). His feet grew to 18.5 in (47 cm) long. So, he **clinched** the tallest man and largest feet records!

WCLE

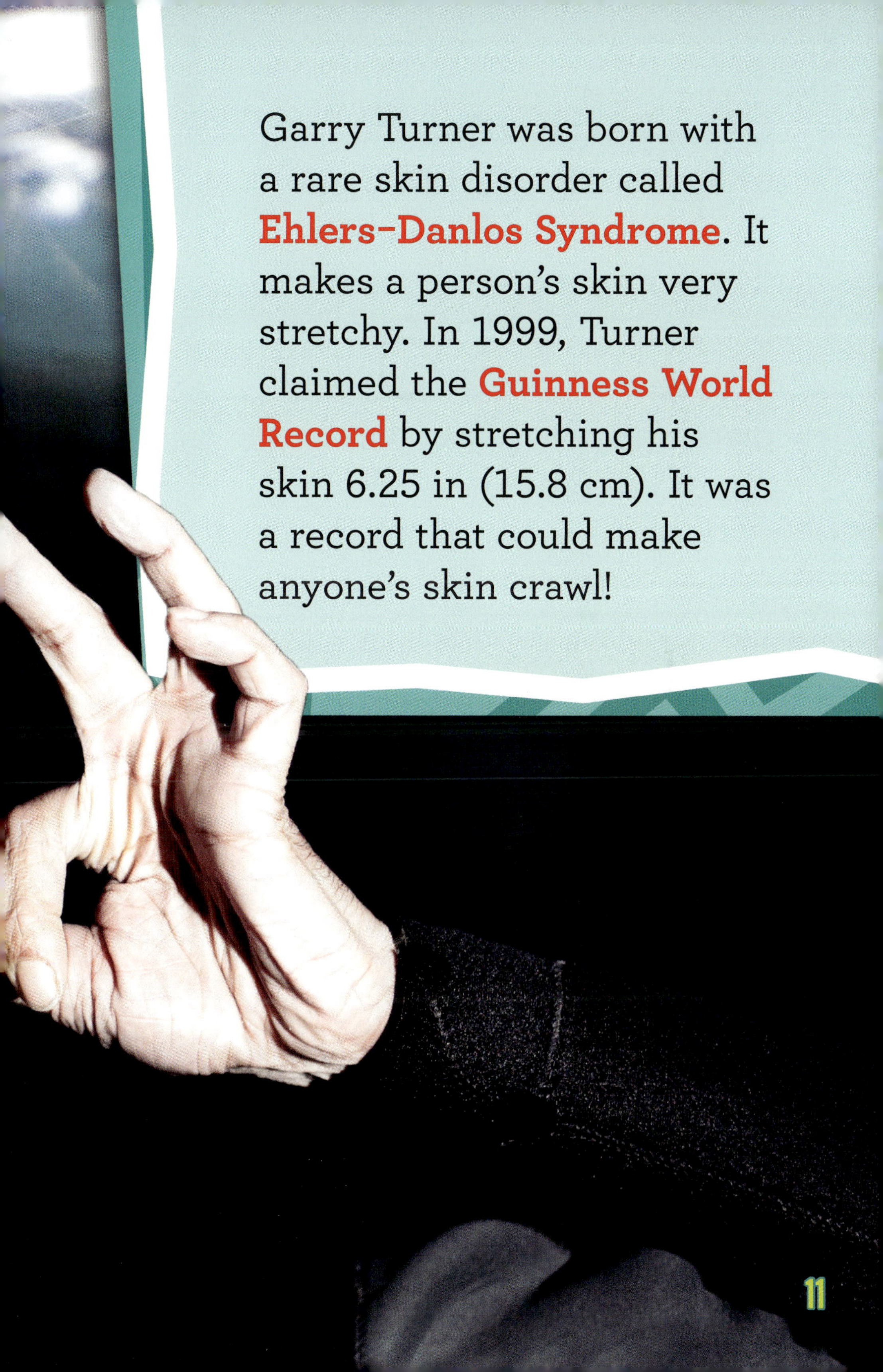

Garry Turner was born with a rare skin disorder called **Ehlers-Danlos Syndrome**. It makes a person's skin very stretchy. In 1999, Turner claimed the **Guinness World Record** by stretching his skin 6.25 in (15.8 cm). It was a record that could make anyone's skin crawl!

Elaine Davidson got her first piercing in 1997. By 2000, she had 462 to claim the world record for most body piercings! Today, with more than 11,000 piercings, Davidson put a pin in the record!

GUINNESS
WORLD RECORDS

Ram Singh Chauhan started growing his mustache in 1982. In 2011, he was awarded the **Guinness World Record** for longest mustache grown at 14 ft (4.3 m) long.

Martin Tye became **paralyzed** while serving in the British Army. But that did not stop him from claiming the heaviest seated **deadlift** in 2019! Tye was able to lift 1,113 lbs (505 kg).

ICTUS
INVICTUS
GAMES
SURGE

In 2022, Asha Mandela broke her own 2009 record for world's longest **locks** of hair! Beginning in 1982, it took many years to achieve a length of more than 55 feet (17 m)!

FOR THE RECORD

There is no limit to where the human body can go. As far as this collection of world records goes, it is an impressive body of work!

GLOSSARY

clinch – to confirm a win.

deadlift – a lift in weightlifting in which the weight is lifted from the floor to hip level.

Ehlers-Danlos Syndrome – a disorder that affects a person's connective tissue. It causes overly flexible joints and stretchy skin.

Guinness World Record – an award given to those who have broken a record never achieved before.

locks – rope-like strands of hair formed by braiding or locking hair.

paralyzed – affected with a loss of feeling or motion in part of the body.

ONLINE RESOURCES

Booklinks
NONFICTION NETWORK
FREE! ONLINE NONFICTION RESOURCES

To learn more about body records, please visit **abdobooklinks.com** or scan this QR code. These links are routinely monitored and updated to provide the most current information available.

INDEX